THE MAGIC OF LANGUAGE

Prefixes and Suffixes

feathery

unbelievable

colorful

beautiful

By Ann Heinrichs

Published in the United States of America by The Child's World®
PO Box 326, Chanhassen, MN 55317-0326
800-599-READ
www.childsworld.com

Content Adviser:
Kathy Reasy, M.A,
Adjunct Professor,
School of Education,
Dominican University,
River Forest, Illinois

Photo Credits: Cover/frontispiece: Theo Allofs/Corbis. Interior: Corbis: 6 (Charles Gupton), 13 (Laureen March), 15 (Jon Feingersh), 16 (Mike McGill), 17 (Norbert Schaefer), 23 (Martin Harvey/Gallo Images), 26, 28 (Tim Davis); Getty Images/Stone: 5 (Pal Hermansen), 18 (Vincent Besnault); Getty Images/Taxi/Neil McInryre: 11; PhotoEdit: 9 (Michael Newman), 12 (Spencer Grant), 21 (Barbara Stitzer), 24 (Myrleen Ferguson Cate).

The Child's World®: Mary Berendes, Publishing Director

Editorial Directions, Inc.: E. Russell Primm, Editorial Director; Katie Marsico, Project Editor and Line Editor; Matt Messbarger, Editorial Assistant; Susan Hindman, Copyeditor; Sarah E. De Capua and Lucia Raatma, Proofreaders; Peter Garnham, Elizabeth Nellums, Olivia Nellums, Daisy Porter, and Will Wilson, Fact Checkers; Timothy Griffin/IndexServ, Indexer; Cian Loughlin O'Day, Photo Researcher; Linda S. Koutris, Photo Editor

The Design Lab: Kathleen Petelinsek, Art Direction; Kari Thornborough, Page Production

Library of Congress Cataloging-in-Publication Data
Heinrichs, Ann.
 Prefixes and suffixes / by Ann Heinrichs.
    p. cm. — (The magic of language)
 Includes index.
 ISBN 1-59296-431-1 (lib. bdg. : alk. paper)
 1. English language—Suffixes and prefixes—Juvenile literature. I. Title.
 PE1175.H46 2006
 428.1—dc22   2005004003

TABLE OF CONTENTS

CHAPTER ONE

FIND THAT ROOT!

EXAMPLE

There goes a *duckling!* It's diving *underwater.* That's *unbelievable.* What a *fearless* little duck!

See all the white words above? What do you notice about them?

For one thing, they're big words. But you can break those

words into parts. That makes them easy to read!

Each word in the

example has a root.

Duck, water,

believe, and

fear are the roots.

DEFINITION

The **root** is the main part of a word. Letters can be added to the **root** to build new words.

*These little **ducklings** are **fearless!** Of course, they don't know the root words in that sentence are **duck** and **fear.***

As you can see, more letter groups have been added to the roots.

Some come before the root.

Others are at the end. These added letters are called prefixes

and suffixes.

TRY THESE!

What is the **root** in each of these words?

rebuild

teacher

See page 32 for the answers. Don't peek!

QUICK FACT
root

The **root** is sometimes called the base word.

Prefixes and suffixes often change the meaning of the root.

Let's see what they're all about!

$$\frac{2}{10} \text{ of } 40$$

3

This **teacher** is **calling** on a **preteen** student who is very **likeable**.
What are the root words here? **Teach, call, teen,** and **like!**

CHAPTER TWO

WHAT IS A PREFIX?

DEFINITION

A **prefix** is a group of letters added to the beginning of a word.

EXAMPLE

Untie my shoe! **Untangle** my hair!
Unzip my jacket! **Unpack** my bag!

All the white words in the example above use the prefix *un-*. *Un-* changes a word to its opposite. Here are

more examples:

EXAMPLE

Seth is **happy**, but Jared seems **unhappy**.
Frogs are **safe** pets, but alligators are **unsafe**.
If I **roll** up my tongue, can I **unroll** it again?

What are the roots in these examples? **Happy, safe,** and **roll.**

If you add the prefix *-un,* then you make the opposite word!

The prefix *re-* means "to do something over again."

EXAMPLE

**Skippy ate my story. I have to rewrite it.
The storm blew our tree house away. Let's
rebuild it.
Stop jumping on your bed! Remake that bed
right now!**

TRY THESE!

1. Add a **prefix** to these **roots** to create the
   opposite word:
   healthy   even   wise   real   plug

2. Use a **prefix** to create words that mean:
   draw again   tell again   think again
   send again

See page 32 for the answers. Don't peek!

*Not again, Skippy! You ate my story, and I must **rewrite** it. You **disobey** so much, it's **unreal**! I'll **rethink** my plans to take you to Grandma's! Prefixes have been added to **write, obey, real,** and **think.***

CHAPTER THREE

OVER AND UNDER,
BEFORE AND AFTER

EXAMPLE

Stop pouring the milk. My glass is *overflowing!*
Stop feeding me cookies. I don't want to *overeat.*
I'm not pulling any more weeds. I'm *overworked!*

The white words above use the prefix *over-*. Can you see what

over- means in these examples? It means "too much"!

Now let's check out the prefix *under-*. It often means "not enough."

EXAMPLE

This hamburger is still pink. It's **undercooked.**
Don't **underfeed** the octopus. It might start
eating the fish!
I **undercounted** the bunnies. There are ten
instead of seven.

Over- and *under-* can have other meanings, too. They can mean just what they say—"over" and "under"!

Watch out! There's a flock of pigeons overhead.
Are you flying to Ohio? No, we're going overland.
The squirrel buried his nuts underground.
Don't tickle my underarm!

The nut fell from **overhead.** *The squirrel buried it* **underground.**
Now he's in danger of **overeating!** *At least he's not* **underfed.**

*These **preteen** girls are best friends. They will probably still be friends when they're teenagers.*

Let's learn two more easy prefixes. The prefix *pre-* means "before."

Alysha isn't a teenager yet. She's still a preteen.

You can't pay when you get there. You have to prepay.

The prefix *post-* means "after."

Be sure and stay after the game. There's a postgame party!
I'm sorry the holidays are over. I have the postholiday blues.

CHAPTER FOUR

NUMBER PREFIXES

Some prefixes are used to show how many or how much.

EXAMPLE

PREFIX	MEANING
bi-	two
tri-	three
quad-	four
milli-	thousand
semi-	half or partly
multi-	many

*How many wheels does a **bicycle** have? How many folds does a **bifold** wallet have? How many times a month does a **bimonthly** magazine come? Two, of course!*

These examples show words with number prefixes:

A **bicycle** has **two** wheels.

A **tricycle** has **three** wheels.

Quadruplets are **four** brothers or sisters born at the same time.

A **millipede** is a bug that is sometimes called a **thousand**-legger.

A **semicircle** is a **half** circle.

A **multicolored** coat has **many** colors.

TRY THESE!

1. Name a shape that has three sides or angles.

2. What kind of chocolate is only partly sweet?

3. What kind of cereal has many kinds of grain in it?

See page 32 for the answers. Don't peek!

CHAPTER FIVE

GIVE ME A BREAK!

Sometimes you need a break between the prefix and the root. You make that break with a hyphen (-).

When *all-* or *self-* are used as prefixes, they are followed by a hyphen.

EXAMPLE

Don't forget your **all-important** video games.

Skippy plays, works, and protects us. He's an **all-purpose** dog.

My teacher seems to have **all-seeing** eyes.

Maria has a lot of **self-respect**.

How did you learn to play checkers? I'm **self-taught**.

Grandma has a **self-cleaning** oven.

*For a **self-taught** checker player, this boy is pretty good! But his **all-knowing** friend has probably guessed his next move.*

A prefix before a proper noun needs a hyphen, too.

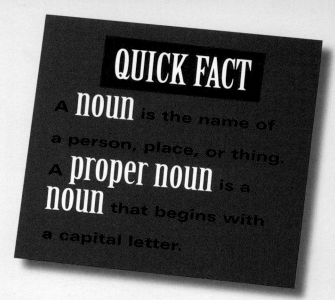

EXAMPLE

School won't be out until **mid-June**.
I saw **ex-President** Jimmy Carter on TV.
We got skateboards at the **pre-Christmas** sale.

*It's only **mid-May**, and these **self-confident** girls already have their **all-important** skateboards out!*

*How many words with prefixes can describe these kids? They **disagree.** They're being **unfriendly.** They **misunderstand** each other. They're **nonexperts** at solving their problems. Can you think of any more?*

Want More?

Here are some more prefixes and their meanings:

PREFIX	MEANING	EXAMPLE
trans-	across	trans-Atlantic
non-	not	nonsticky
dis-	opposite of	disagree
mis-	wrongly	misjudge
de-	remove	declaw

CHAPTER SIX

WHAT IS A SUFFIX?

DEFINITION

A **suffix** is a group of letters added to the end of a word.

Suppose the root is a verb, or action word. Do you want to know who's doing the action? Just add the suffix *-er* to the end. That changes the verb into a noun.

*This **baker** is mixing dough so he can **bake** bread.*
*The verb **bake** is the root word in this sentence.*

My turtle can eat ten strawberries a day. He's a good eater.

Mr. Yee will teach us some Chinese. He's a great teacher.

Here's another way to change verbs into nouns. Just add the suffix -ment.

I like the way you move when you dance. Can you teach me that movement?

Our leaders govern us. They make up our government.

Justin likes to amaze people. He likes to see the amazement on their faces.

Let's try something else with verbs. Try adding the suffix -able.

That changes the verb into an adjective.

It's easy to like Tweety. He's a likeable bird.

Fluffy can't do a backflip. That's not a doable trick.

Yuk! I can't drink that cherry soda. It's just not drinkable!

CHAPTER SEVEN

MORE SUFFIXES

T he suffix *-ful* changes a verb into an adjective.

QUICK FACT An *adjective* is a word that modifies, or describes, a *noun.*

EXAMPLE

Elephants love to **play**. They are **playful** animals.
I can **use** that rubber chicken. It will be **useful** at Gina's party.
Matt always tries to **help** people. He's very **helpful** to Grandpa.

The suffix *-less* means "without."

EXAMPLE

Are you tired of eating **sugar**? Then try this **sugarless** gum.
A tree fell on the beaver's **home**. Now the beaver is **homeless**.
I'm too excited to **sleep**. I guess I'll have a **sleepless** night.

You can use the suffixes *-ful* and *-less* to create opposite words.

Just look:

EXAMPLE

I'm hopeful about the game but hopeless about my grades.

Kevin is careful with money but careless with his mittens.

What shall I paint? Flowers are colorful, but air is colorless.

*This girl is **hopeful** she won't have a **sleepless** night as long as her **faithful** bear is with her. What are the root words? **Hope**, **sleep**, and **faith**.*

The suffix -*y* comes in handy for making adjectives, too.

**Stop tracking mud in the house! Get those
muddy boots out of here!
I like to snuggle in Scooter's fur. He's very furry.
Want to have fun?
Watch a chimpanzee
do funny tricks!**

The suffix -*ly* turns an adjective

into an adverb. Add the suffix -*ness* to

the same root, and you have a noun!

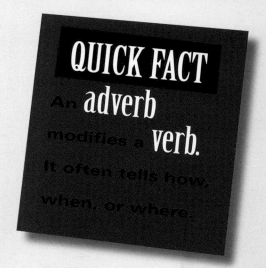

QUICK FACT
An *adverb*
modifies a *verb.*
It often tells how,
when, or where.

ADJECTIVE	ADVERB	NOUN
close	closely	closeness
happy	happily	happiness
kind	kindly	kindness
lazy	lazily	laziness
fuzzy	fuzzily	fuzziness

These **furry** *chimpanzees are* **playful.**
They're doing **funny** *tricks.*

HOT TIP

If the root ends with -e, you often drop the -e when adding a suffix. If the root ends with -y, you often change the -y to -i when adding a suffix.

*Oops! This boy made a **foolish** mistake!*

Want More?

Here are even more suffixes and their uses:

SUFFIX	WHAT IT DOES	EXAMPLE
-ous	changes a noun to an adjective	fame famous
-ish	changes a noun to an adjective	fool foolish
-tion	changes a verb to a noun	create creation
-ize	changes a noun to a verb	vapor vaporize
-ify	changes an adjective to a verb	false falsify
-hood	changes a noun to a new noun	child childhood

CHAPTER EIGHT

WHEN SMILES ARE SMILING, CUTE GETS CUTER

Some suffixes change a verb into different verb forms. Those suffixes are *-s, -es, -d, -ed,* and *-ing.*

EXAMPLE

When Melissa starts to smile, her dog starts smiling, too.
Wilbur barks all day. Last night, he barked till midnight.

Adjectives and adverbs use the suffixes *-er* and *-est* to compare things.

EXAMPLE

Turtles are cute, frogs are cuter, and kittens are the cutest of all.
Mice run fast, monkeys run faster, and tigers run the fastest of all.

CHAPTER NINE

BIG WORDS?
NO PROBLEM!

Want to make some big words? Just try adding two suffixes

to a root!

EXAMPLE

ROOT	+	SUFFIX	+	SUFFIX	=	BIG WORD
hope		*-less*		*-ness*		hopelessness
care		*-ful*		*-ly*		carefully
kind		*-ly*		*-ness*		kindliness
cheer		*-ful*		*-ness*		cheerfulness
amaze		*-ing*		*-ly*		amazingly

TRY THESE!

Make big words by adding two **suffixes** to the **root.**

ROOT	+	SUFFIX	+	SUFFIX
power		-less		-ness
use		-ful		-ness
joy		-ful		-ly
fool		-ish		-ness

See page 32 for the answers. Don't peek!

This girl is *cheerfully* giving someone a present. Aren't you amazed at her **kindliness?** She is **hopelessly** generous! See what big words you can make using two suffixes.

CHAPTER TEN

MAKING WORD SANDWICHES

S peaking of big words, how about building a word sandwich?

Here's how it works:

*Pigs flying? That's **unbelievable**! They might find flying **disagreeable**!*

Put the root in the middle. The root is like the meat. Put a prefix

in the front and a suffix at the end. They are like two slices of bread.

Presto! Word sandwich!

EXAMPLE

PREFIX +	ROOT +	SUFFIX =	WORD SANDWICH
un-	believe	*-able*	unbelievable
non-	break	*-able*	nonbreakable
dis-	agree	*-able*	disagreeable
self-	improve	*-ment*	self-improvement
re-	attach	*-ment*	reattachment
mis-	manage	*-ment*	mismanagement

These words are really big—like big, fat hamburgers! But you can

read them easily now. That's because you can break those words apart.

Don't try this with your hamburger, though!

At the Library

Bridgman, Beth. *Prefixes, Bases, and Suffixes.* London: Usborne Books, 1999.

Cerf, Christopher. *The Un People Versus the Re People.* London: Golden Books Publishing, 2000.

Draze, Dianne. *Red Hot Root Words: Mastering Vocabulary with Prefixes, Suffixes, and Root Words.* San Luis Obispo, Calif.: Dandy Lion Publications, 2000.

On the Web

Visit our home page for lots of links about grammar:

http://www.childsworld.com/links

NOTE TO PARENTS, TEACHERS, AND LIBRARIANS: We routinely check our Web links to make sure they're safe, active sites—so encourage your readers to check them out!

Through the Mail or by Phone

To find the answer to a grammar question, contact:

THE GRAMMAR HOTLINE DIRECTORY
Tidewater Community College Writing Center, Building B205
1700 College Crescent
Virginia Beach, VA 23453
Telephone: (757) 822-7170

NATIONWIDE GRAMMAR HOTLINE
University of Arkansas at Little Rock, English Department
2801 South University Avenue
Little Rock, AR 72204-1099
Telephone: (501) 569-3161

Fun with Prefixes and Suffixes

Complete the boldfaced words in these sentences by adding prefixes or suffixes.

1. Shaking the beehive was a **fool____** idea.

2. That music is too **nois____** ! I'm going to **____plug** the stereo.

3. You agreed with me yesterday. Why are you **____agree____** with me today?

4. Mr. Sheets is **____able** to chew a carrot. He's **complete____ tooth____** .

5. Pens are **use____** , but if they're out of ink, they are **use____** .

6. That giraffe arrived on a **____Atlantic** flight from Africa.

7. My puppy was happy this morning, but now he seems **____happy.**

See page 32 for the answers. Don't peek!

Answers

Answers to Text Exercises

page 6
plug, build, teach, drink

page 8
1. unhealthy, uneven, unwise, unreal, unplug
2. redraw, retell, rethink, resend

page 14
1. triangle
2. semisweet
3. multigrain

page 26
1. powerlessness
2. usefulness
3. joyfully
4. foolishness

Answers to Fun with Prefixes and Suffixes

1. foolish
2. noisy, unplug
3. disagreeing
4. unable, completely, toothless
5. useful, useless
6. trans-Atlantic
7. unhappy

About the Author

Ann Heinrichs was lucky. Every year from grade three through grade eight, she had a big, fat grammar textbook and a grammar workbook. She feels that this prepared her for life. She is now the author of more than 180 books for children and young adults. She has also enjoyed successful careers as a children's book editor and an advertising copywriter. Ann grew up in Fort Smith, Arkansas, and lives in Chicago, Illinois.